The Art of Brian Hollins

SKETCH PAGE

The Art of Brian Hollins

www.brianhollinsart.com

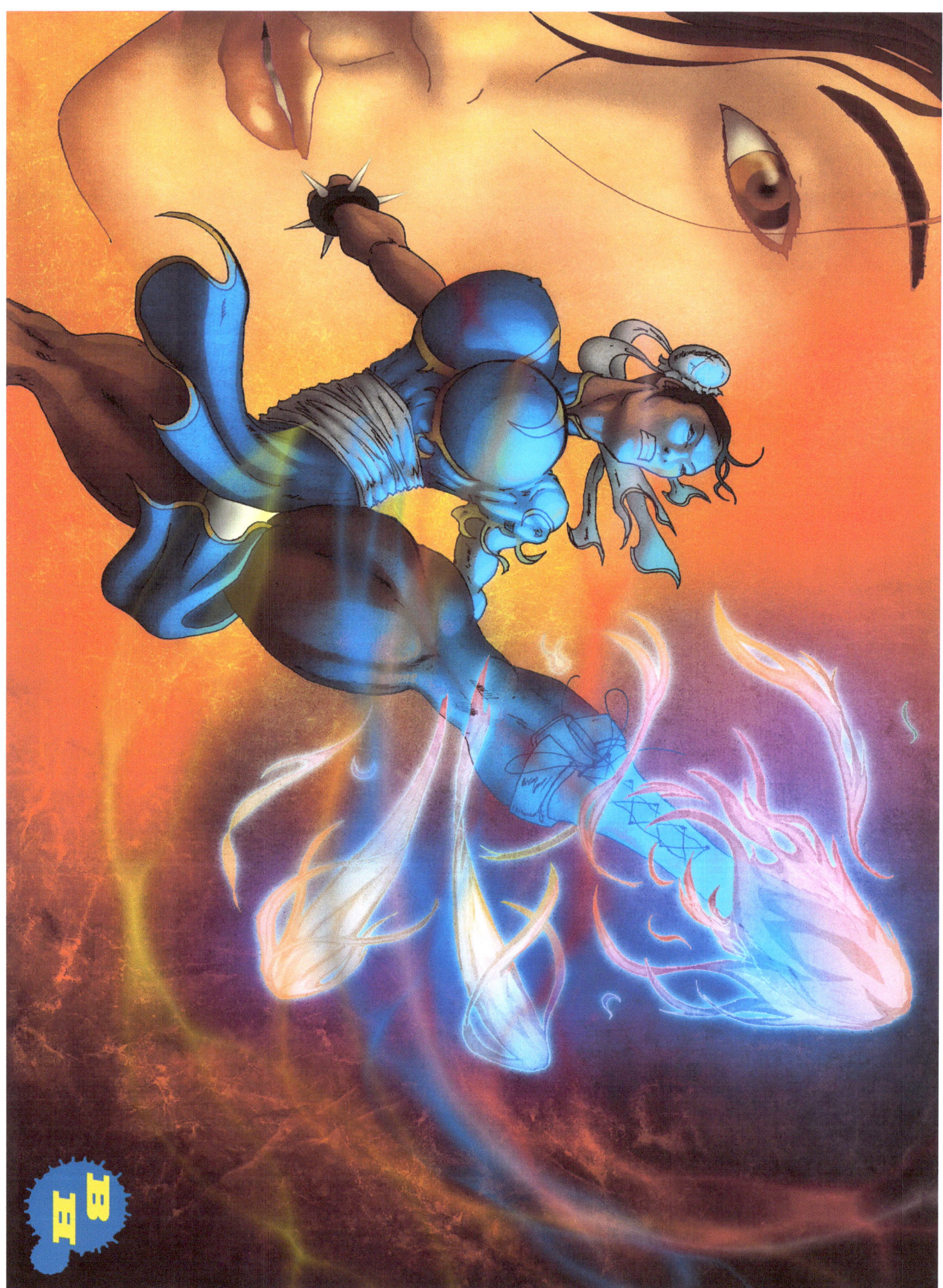

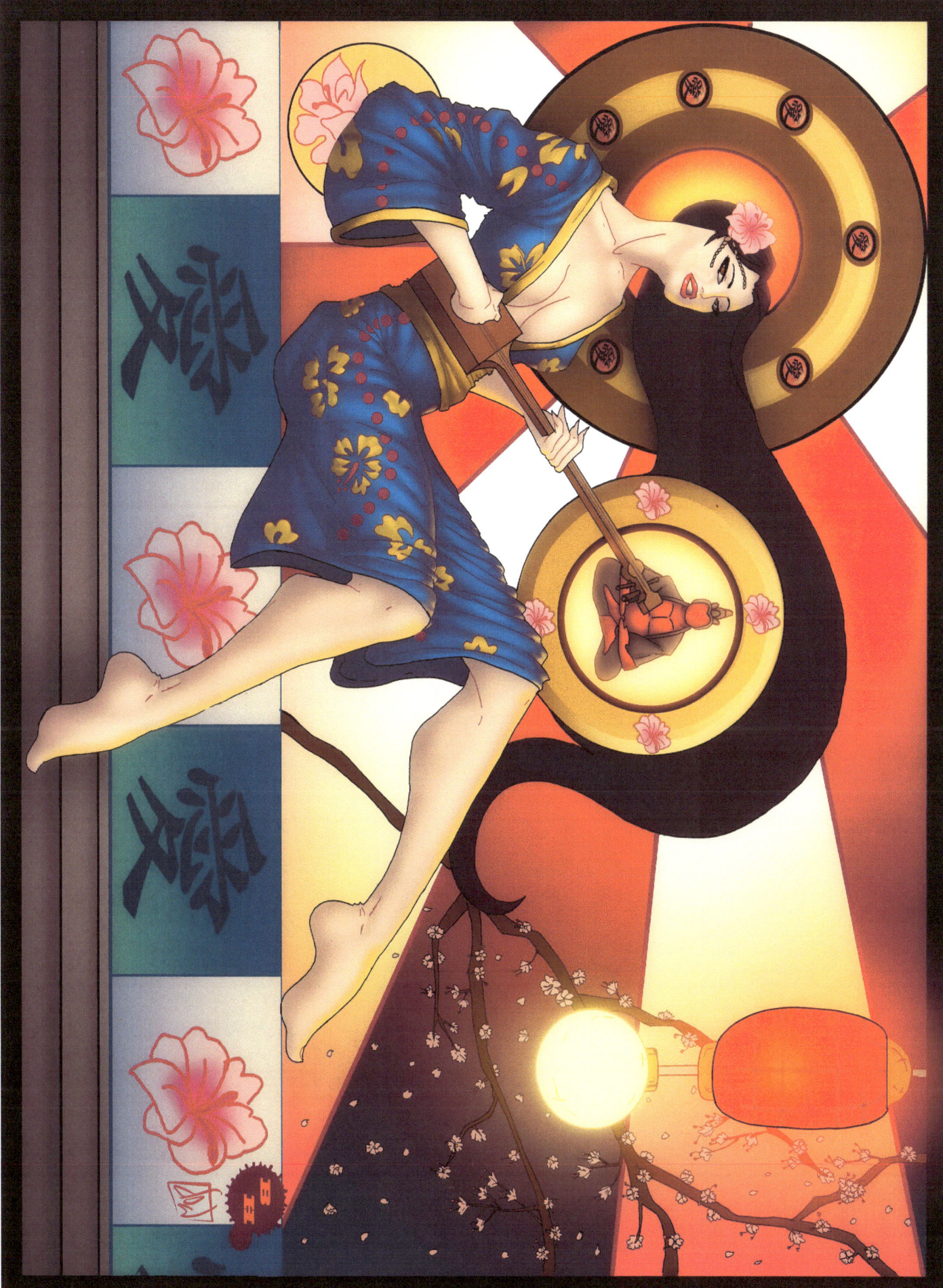

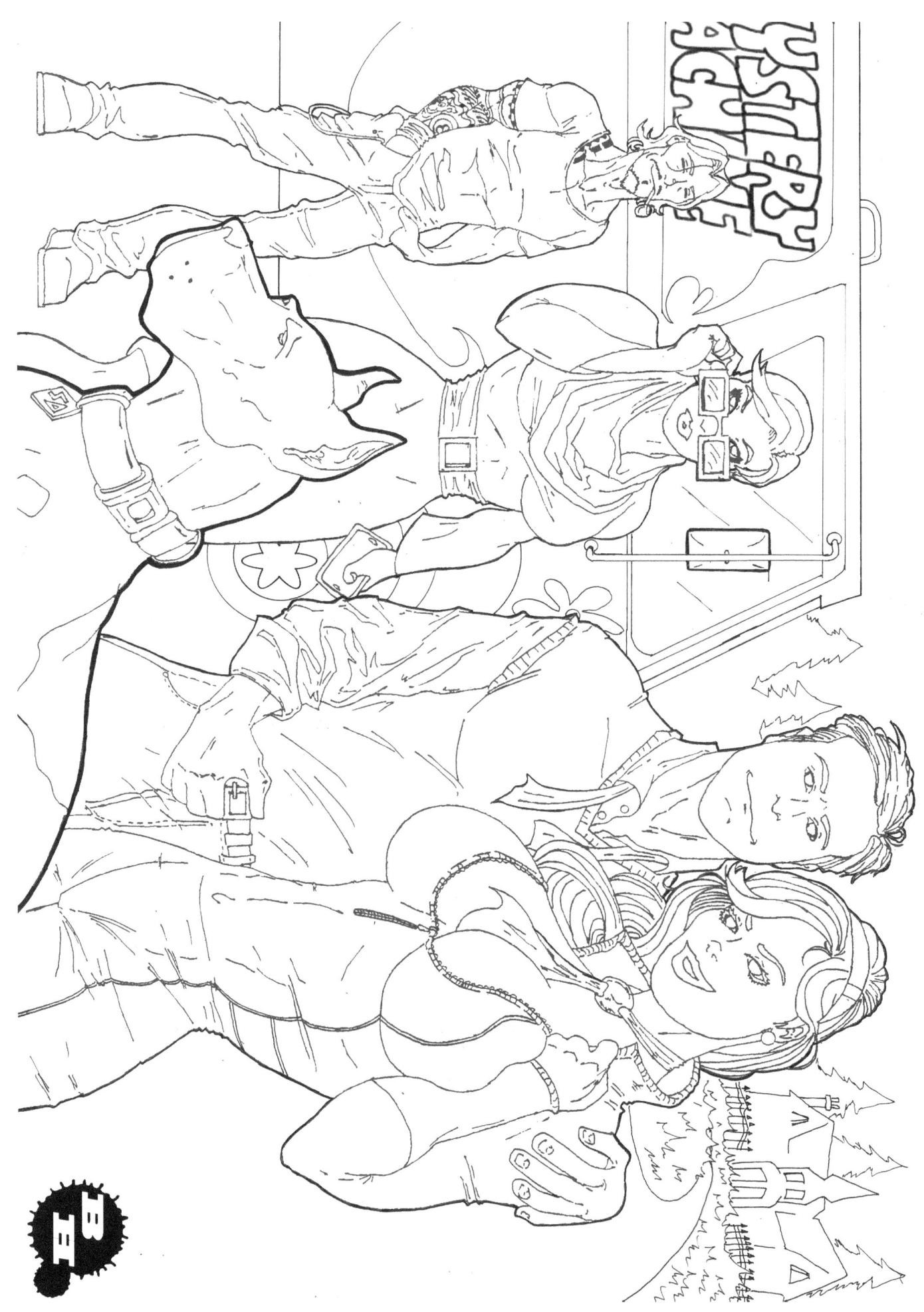

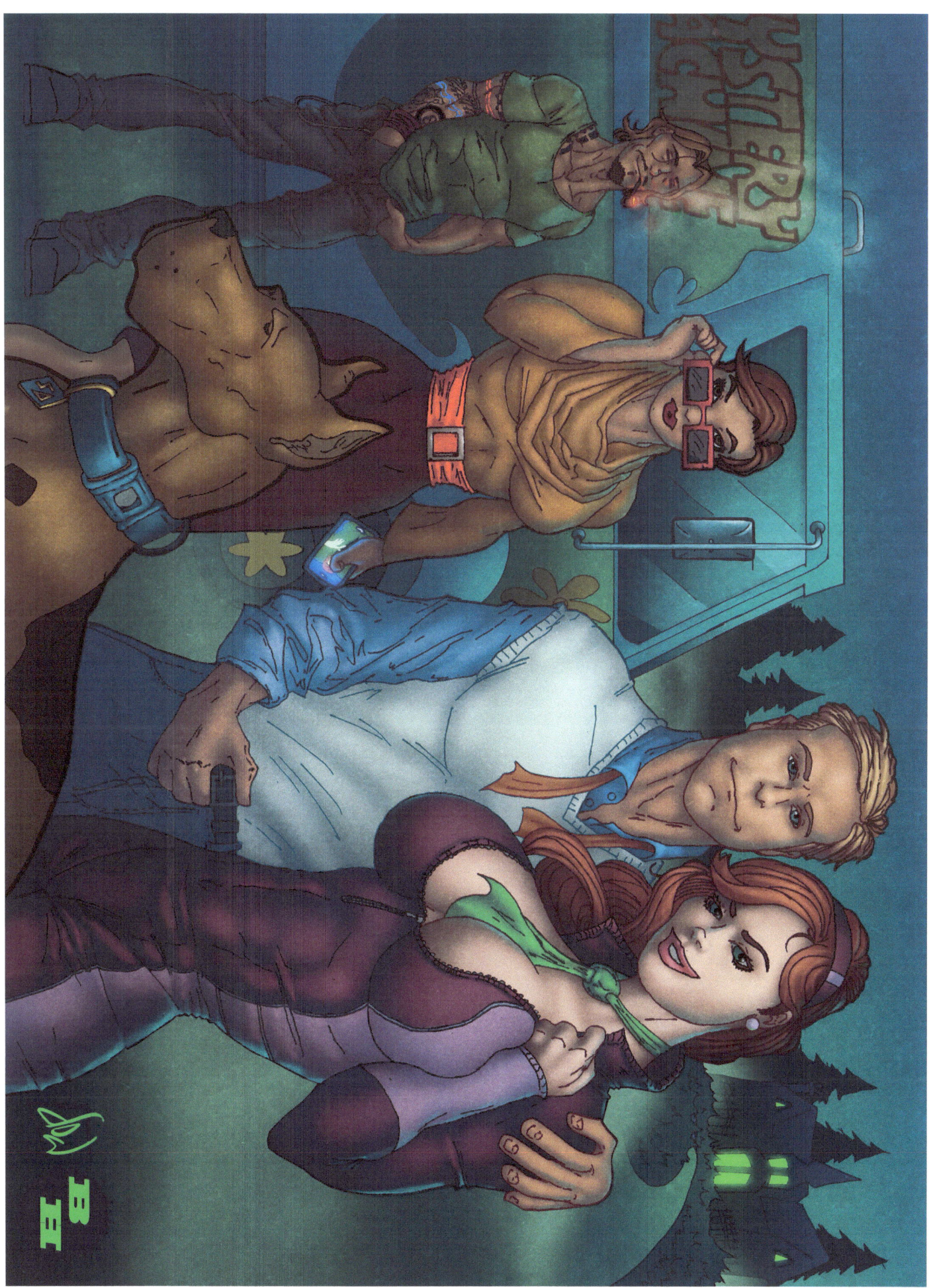

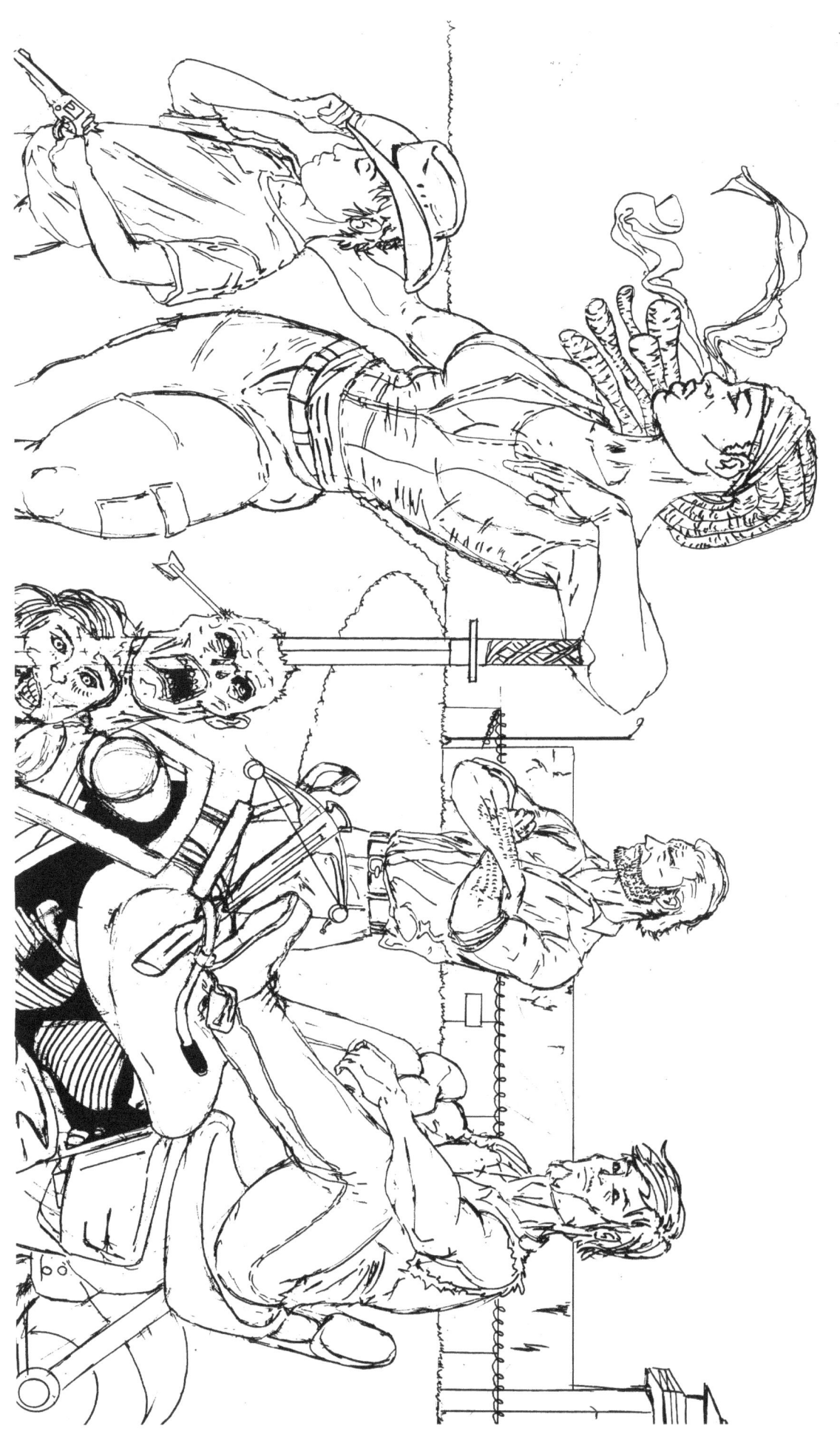

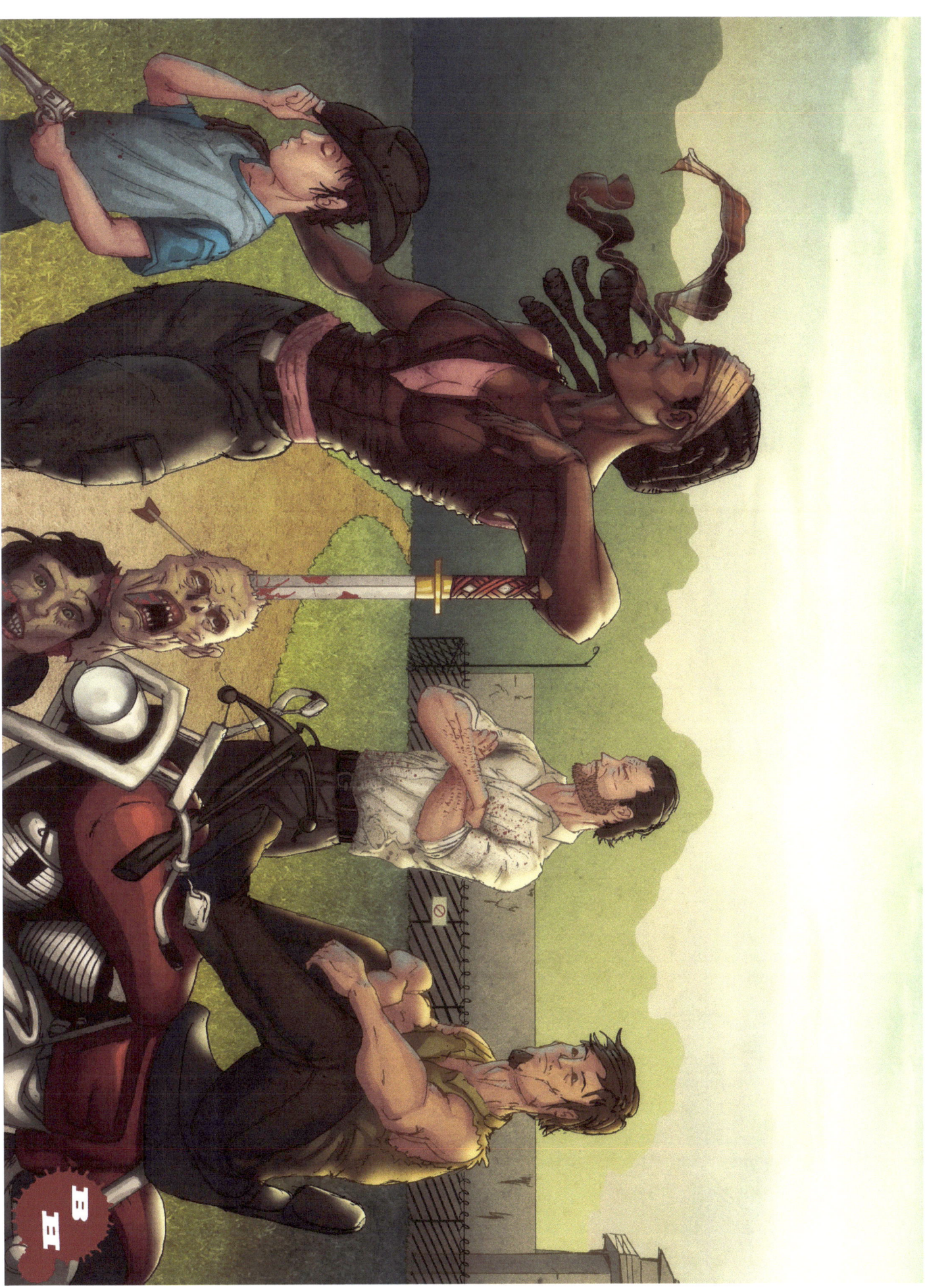

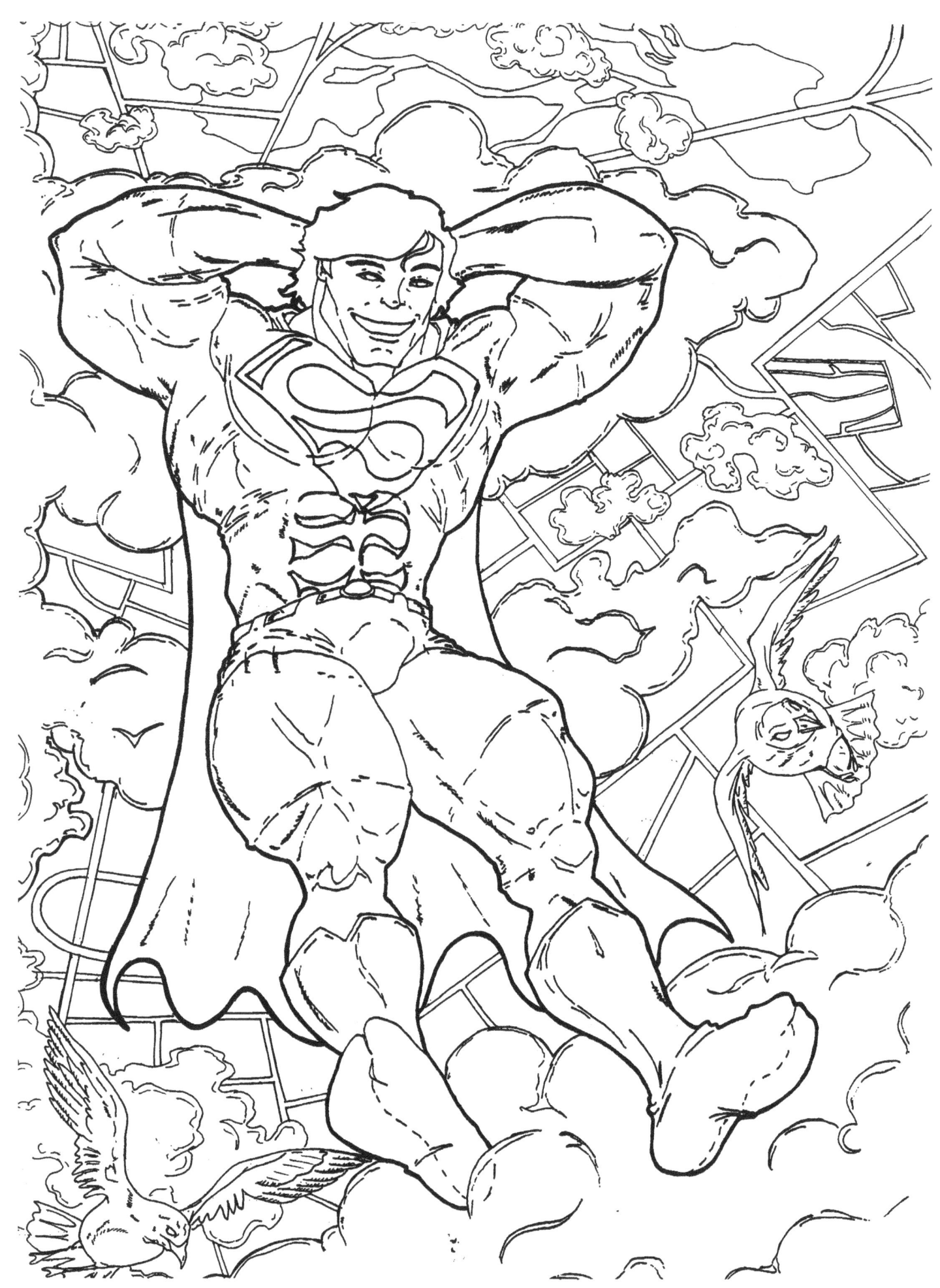

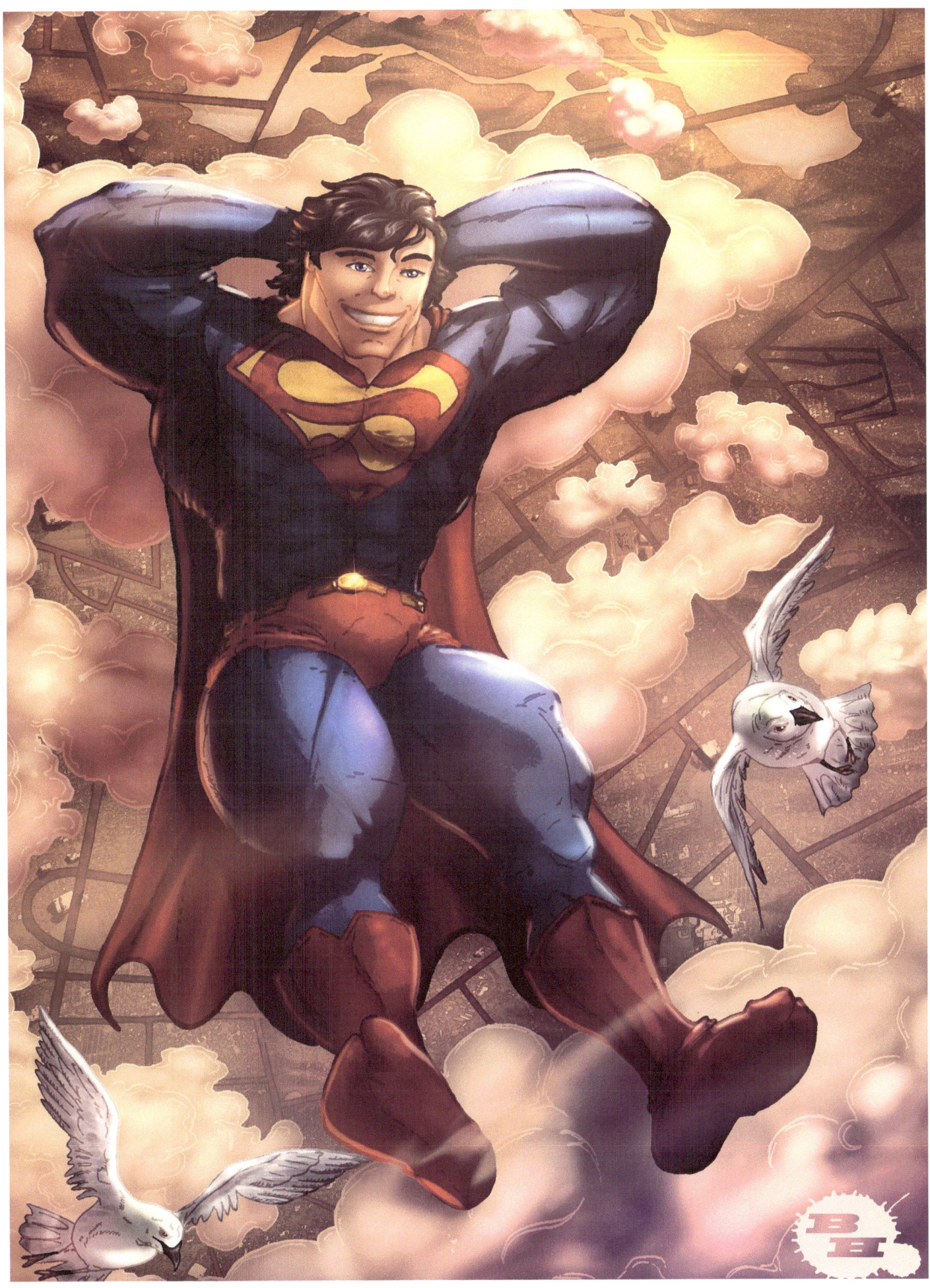

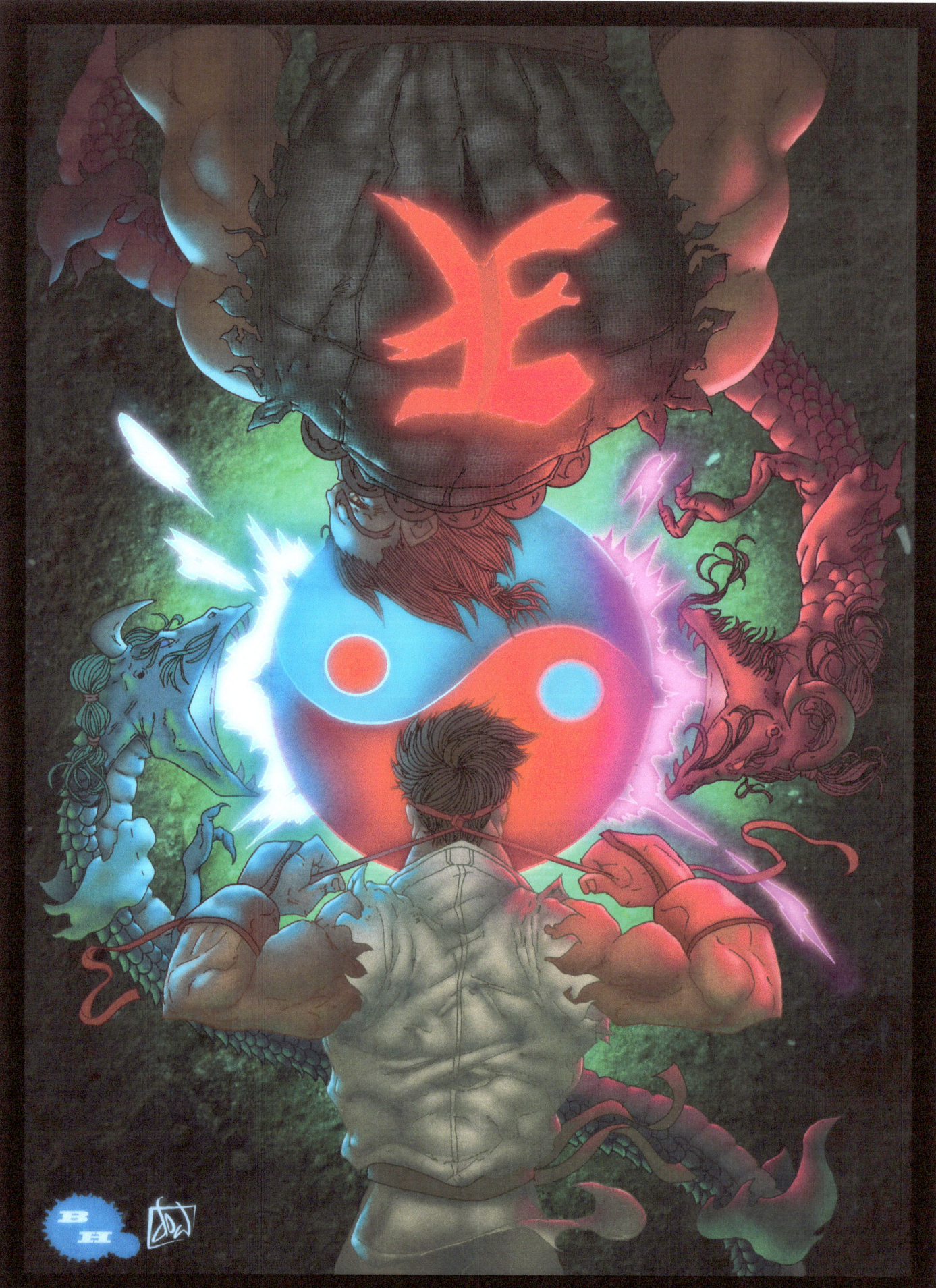

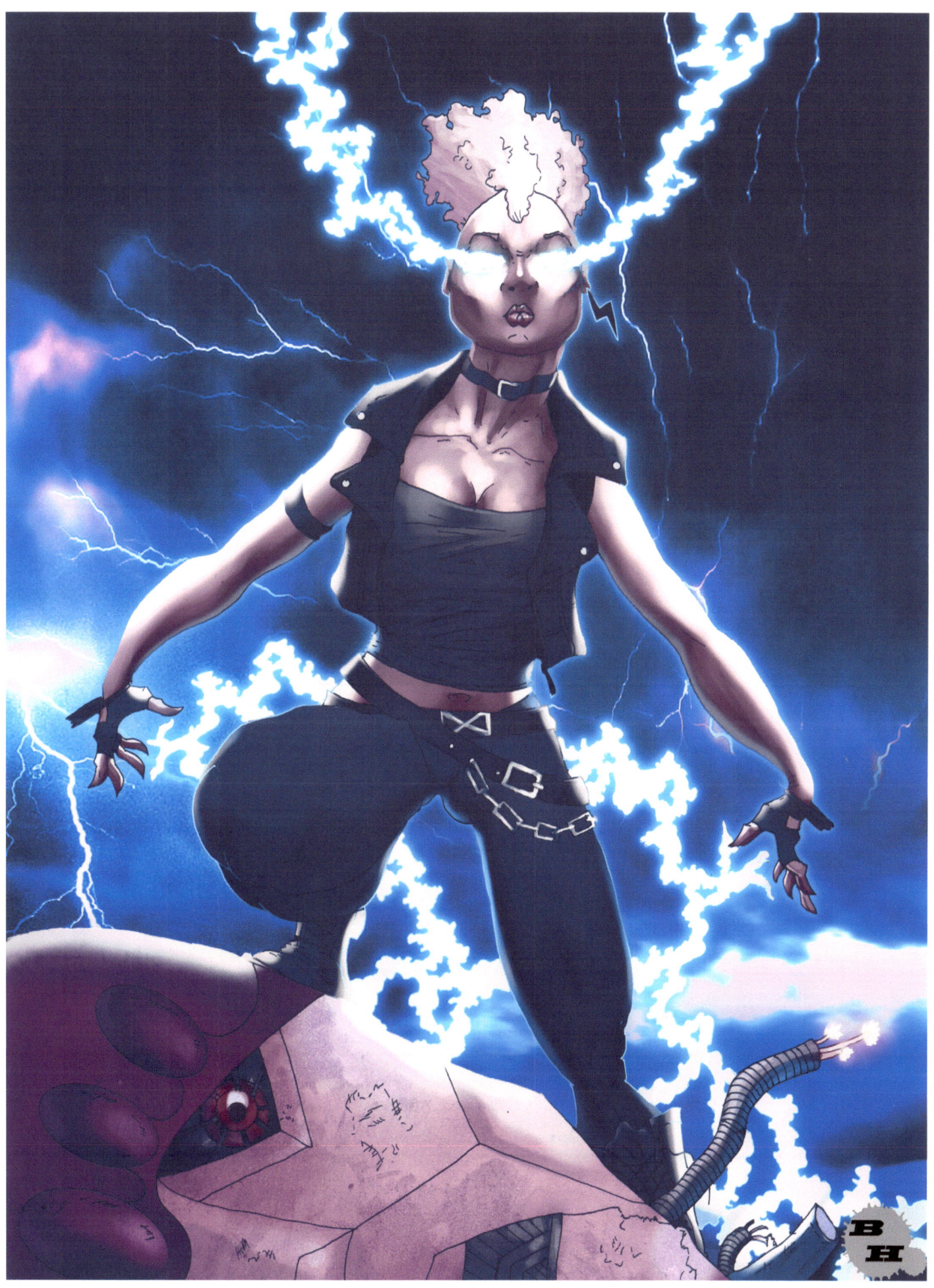

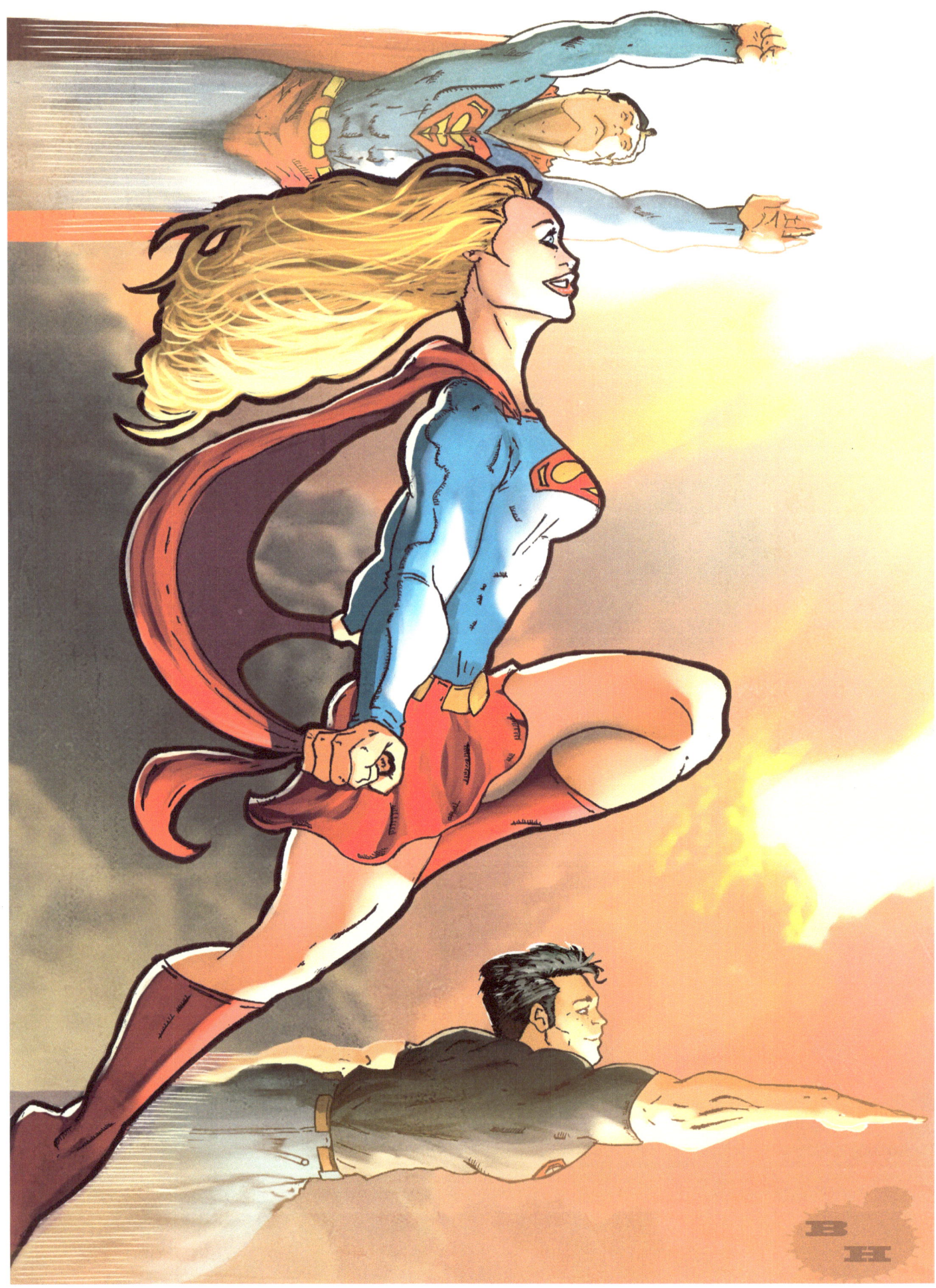

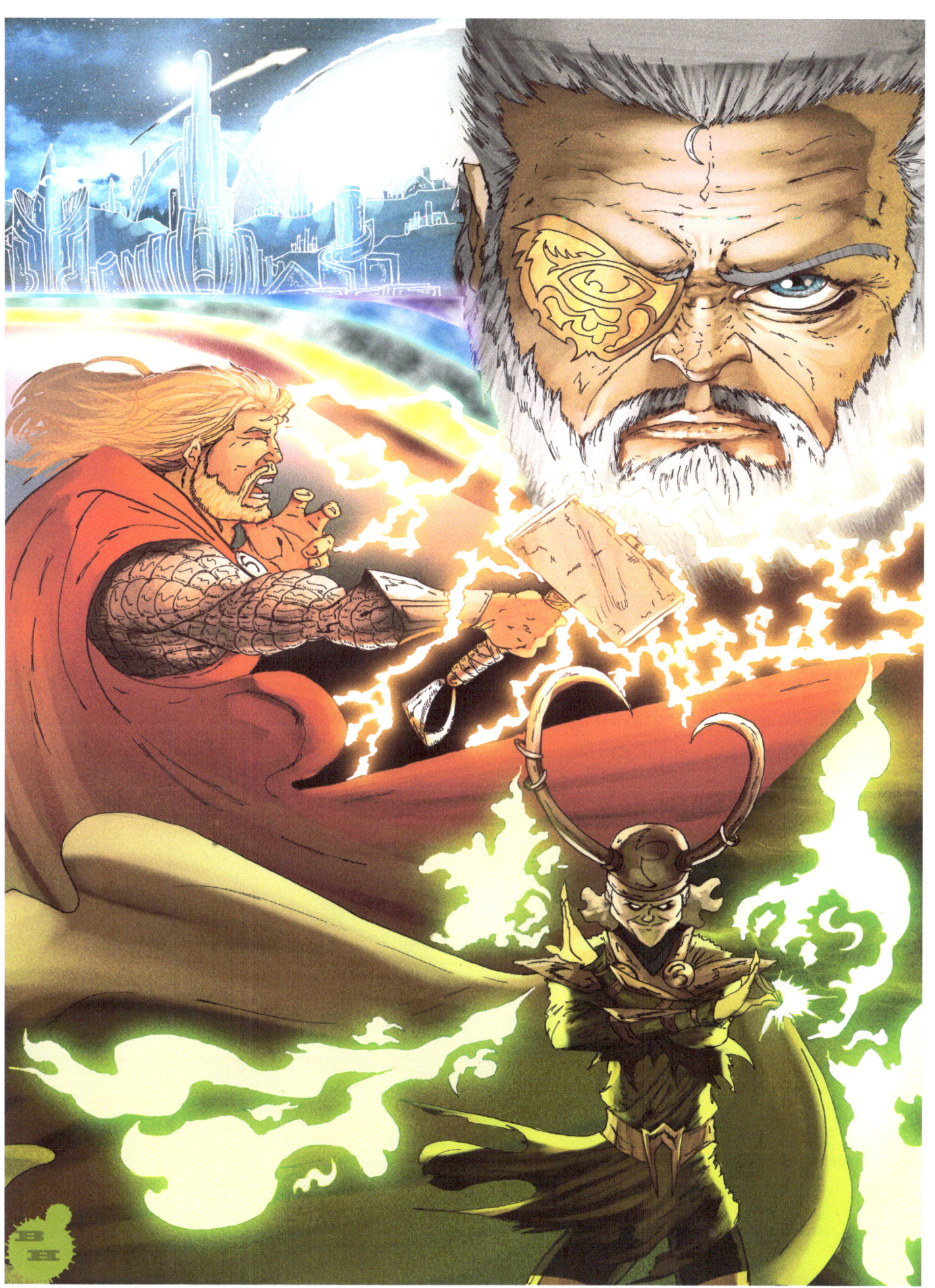

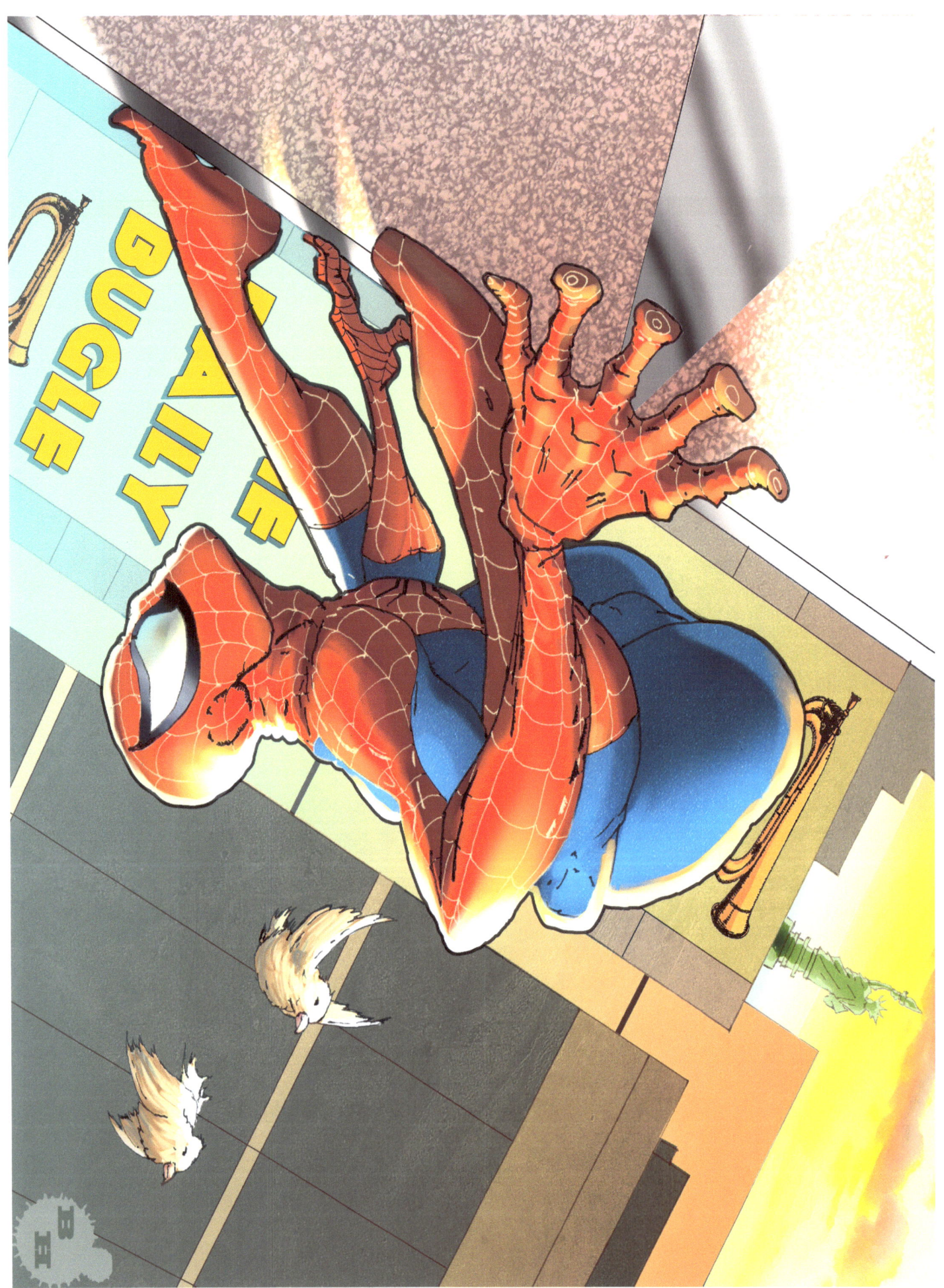

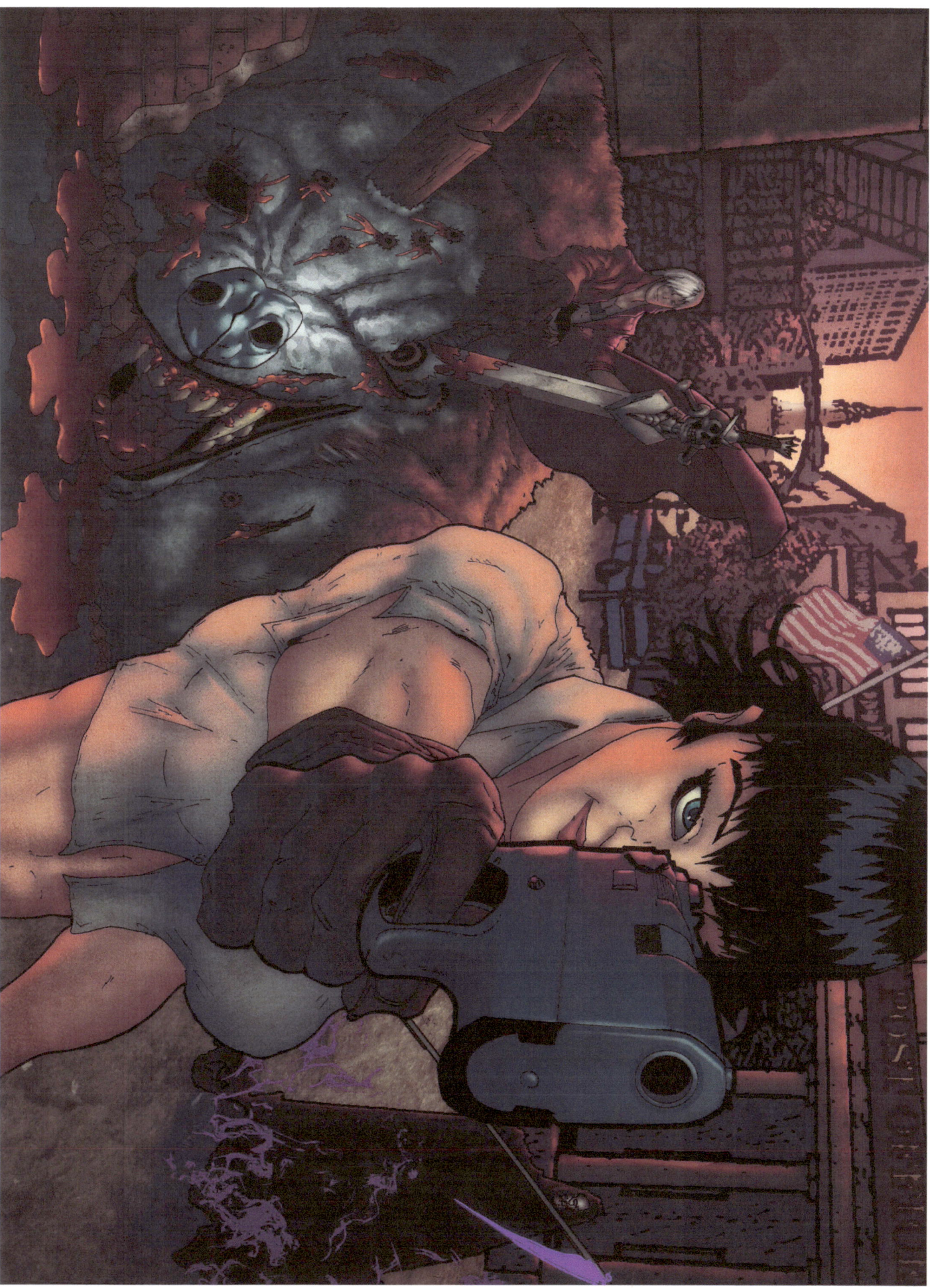

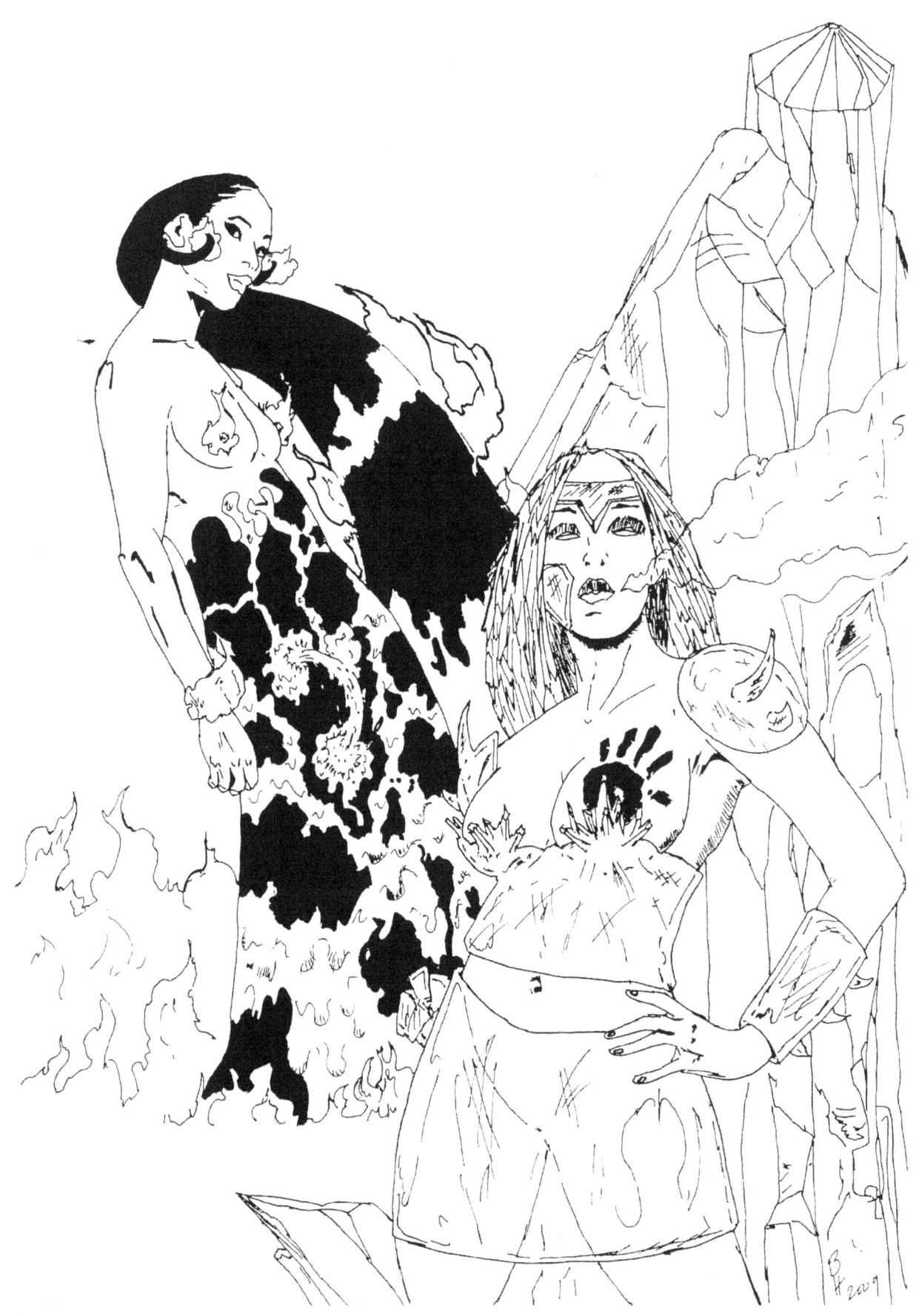

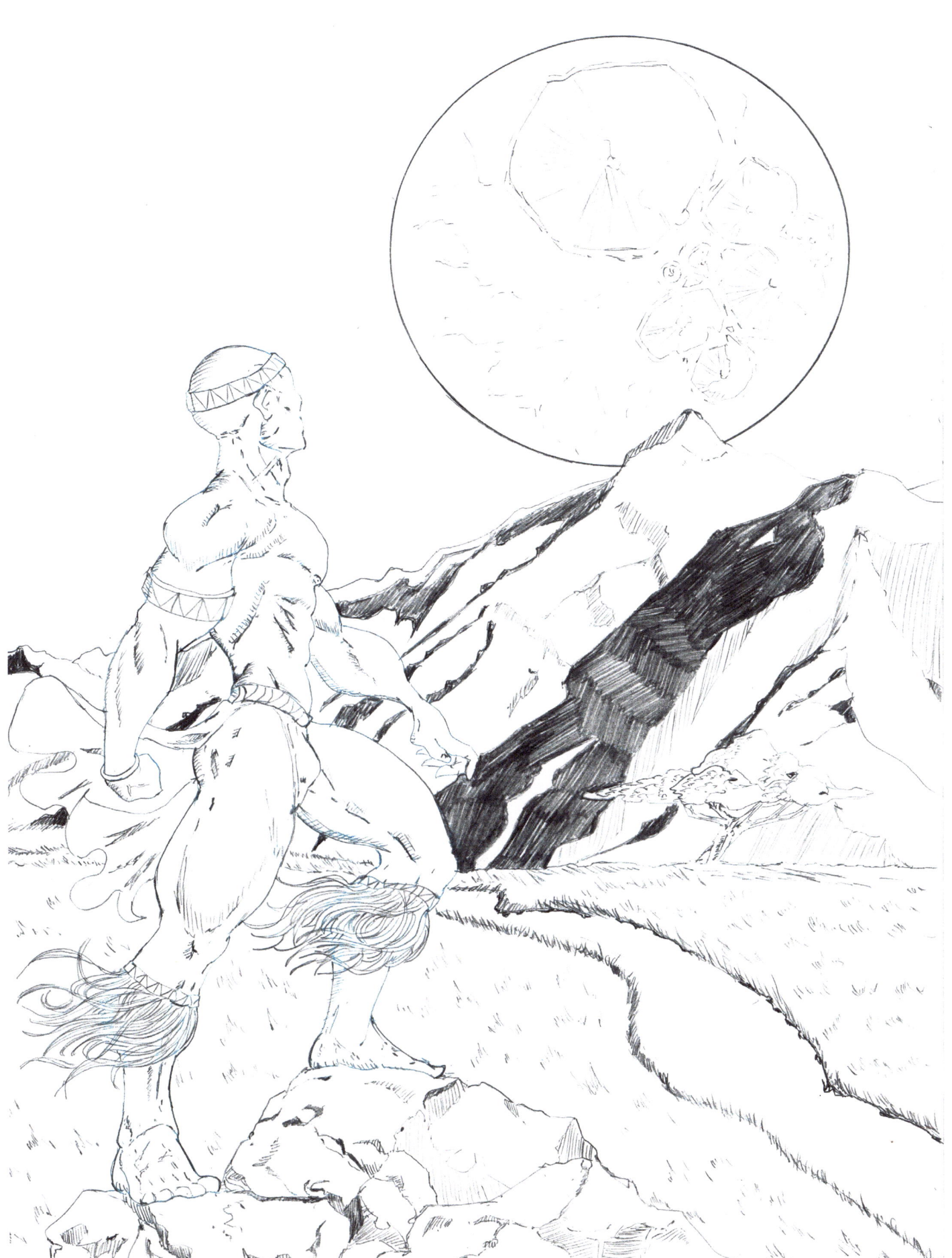

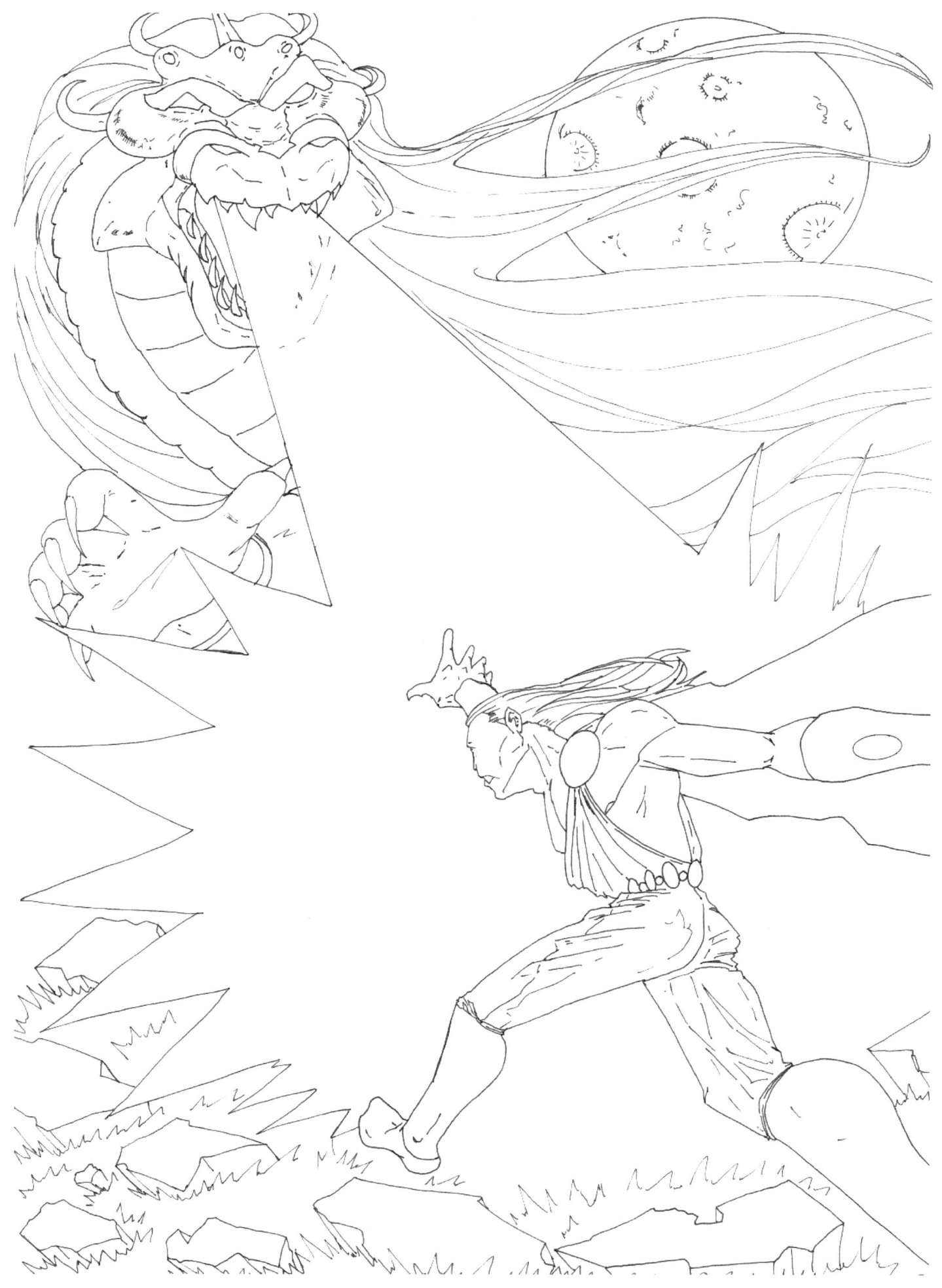

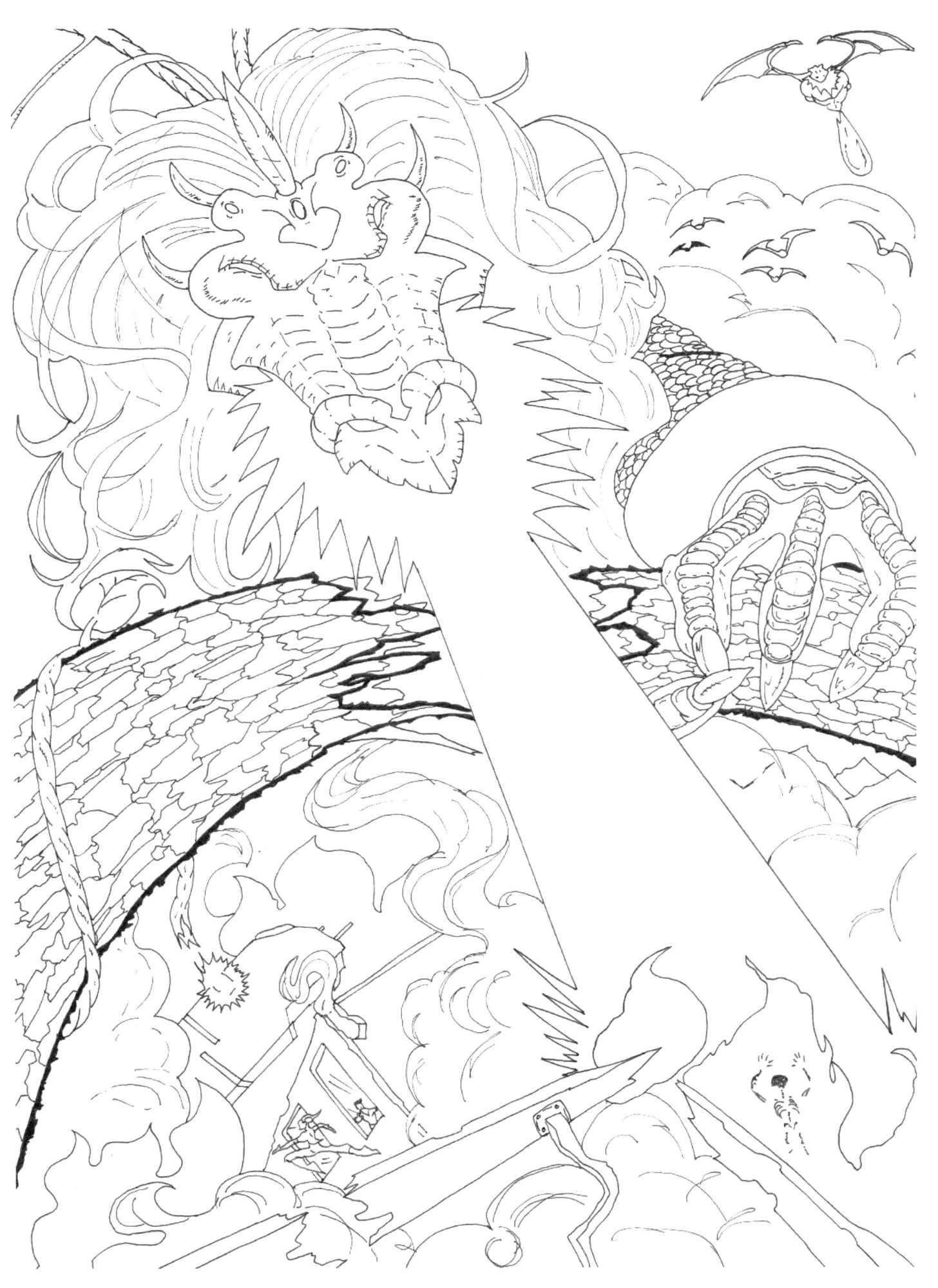

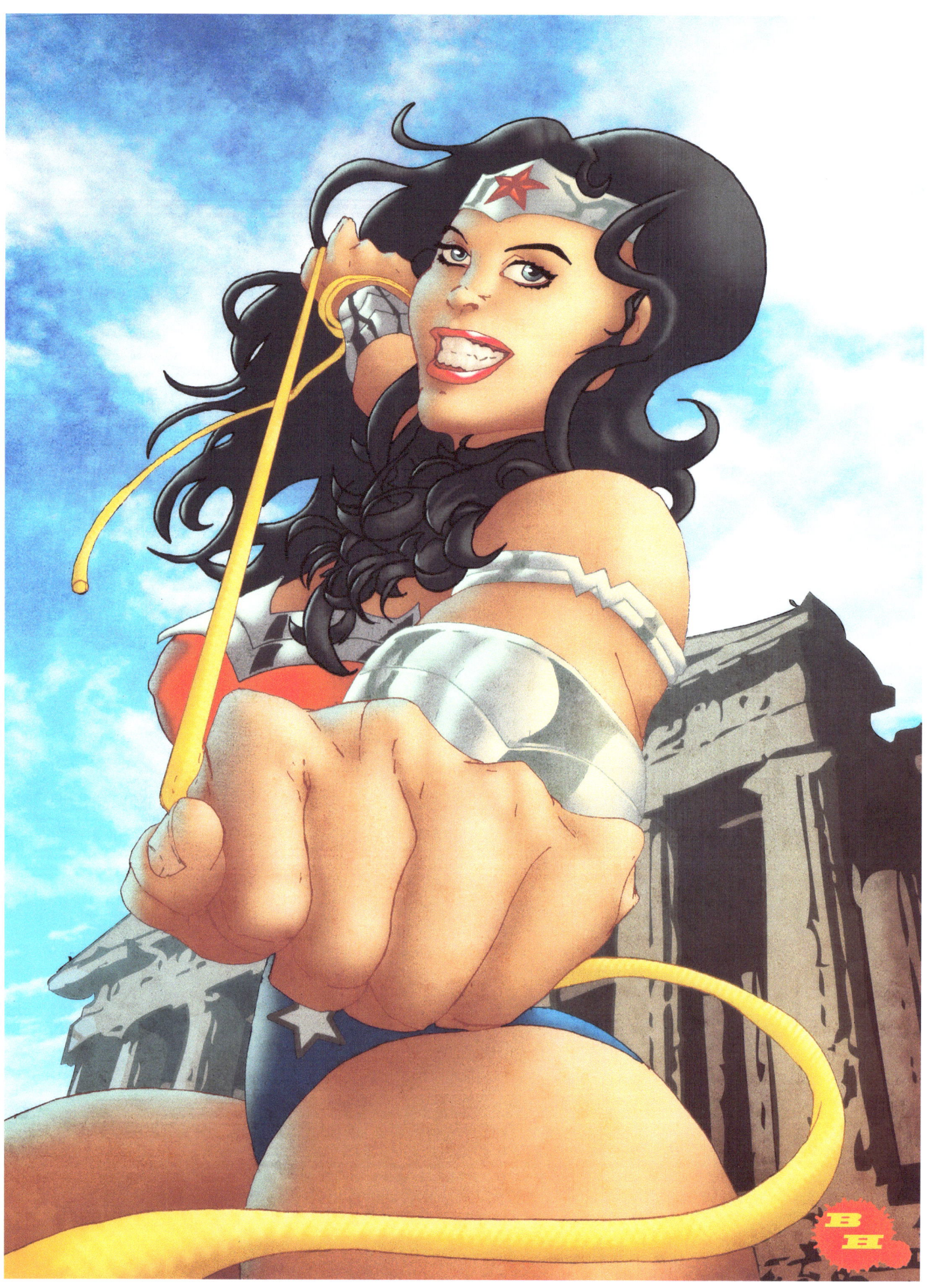

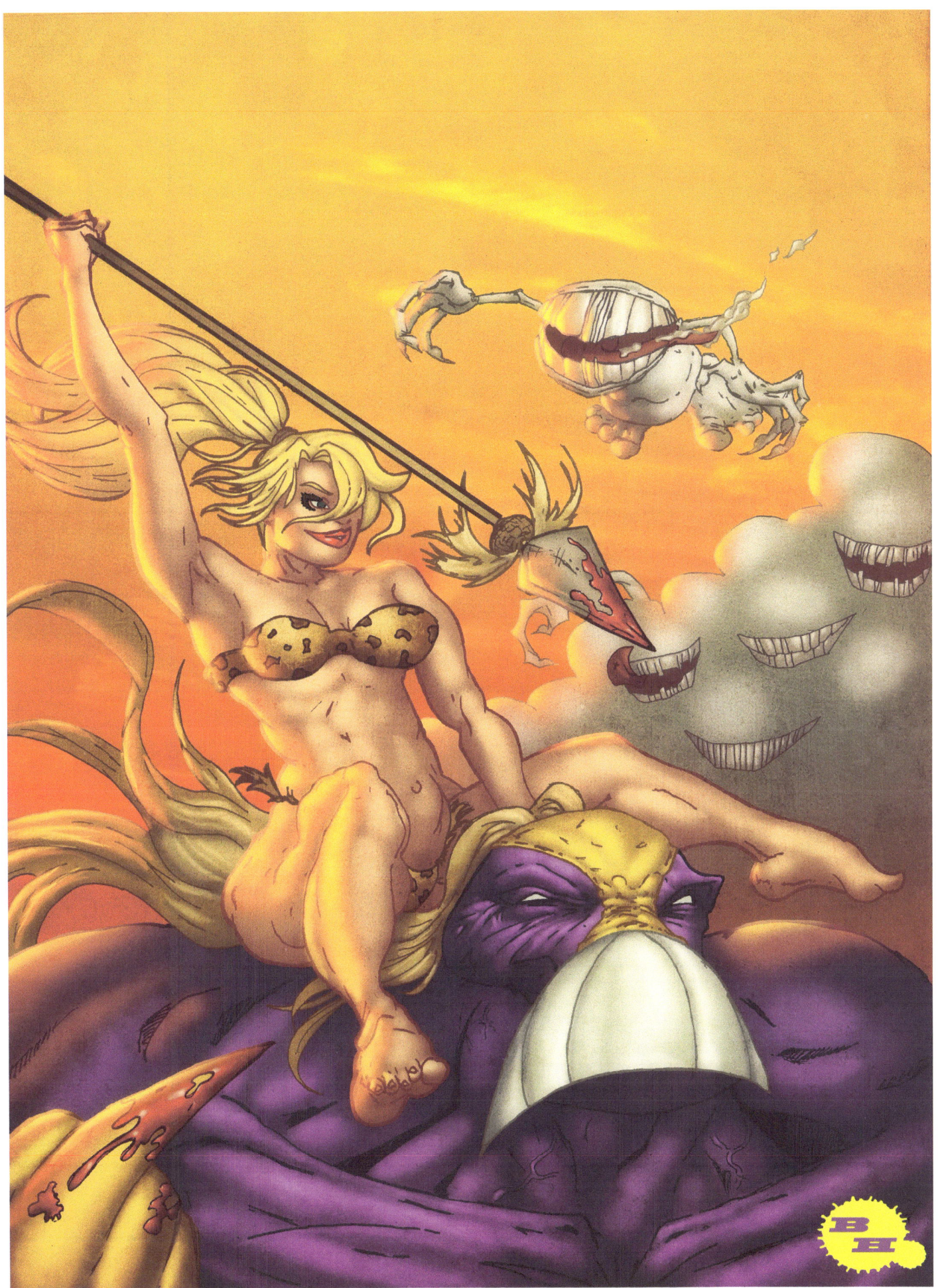

www.ingramcontent.com/pod-product-compliance
Lightning Source LLC
Chambersburg PA
CBHW050439180526
45159CB00006B/2594